PEOPLE FOR PUGET SOUND

FIELD GUIDE

to the

GEODUCK

David George Gordon

SASQUATCH BOOKS
Seattle

Printed in the United States of America.

Cover design and illustration: Dugald Stermer
Interior illustrations: Jim Hays
Composition: grafx

Library of Congress Cataloging-in-Publication Data

Gordon, David G. (David George), 1950–
    Field guide to the geoduck / David George Gordon.
        p. cm. — (Sasquatch field guide series)
    At head of title: People for Puget Sound.
    Includes bibliographical references.
    ISBN 1-57061-045-2
    1. Geoduck I. People for Puget Sound. II. Title. III. Series.
    QL430.7.H53G67 1996   95-48277
    594'.11 — dc20   CIP

Sasquatch Books
1008 Western Avenue
Seattle, Washington 98104
(206) 467-4300

Sales of this field guide help support People for Puget Sound, a nonprofit organization dedicated to the preservation of water quality and natural habitats in Puget Sound and the Strait of Juan de Fuca. For information about People for Puget Sound, contact them at 1326 Fifth Avenue, #450, Seattle, WA 98101; (800) PEOPLE2.

Contents

Introduction

According to the Suquamish tribe of Washington State, clams have been great gossips since long ago. To silence their incessant chattering and restore peace to the wilderness, the other animals in the Pacific Northwest decided to bury the pesky mollusks on a beach. Today, whenever you walk along the seashore at low tide, you'll see water shooting up from the sand. These spurts come from the deeply buried clams, striving to rid themselves of all the silt and seawater they swallow while continuing to gossip.

Whenever I spy a geoduck clam on a beach, I can't help but think of this centuries-old legend. Judging by the sizable spout from this giant bivalve—the largest burrowing clam in the world—the geoduck must have been quite the blabbermouth in its younger days.

Of course, these incredible creatures have always had plenty to blab about. Not only are they the world's largest burrower, they are also among the longest-lived, with life spans accurately established at well over 140 years. Furthermore, geoducks are among the most abundant clam species on the Northwest Coast. With an estimated population of around 130 million adults, they make up the largest single mass of marine animals in Washington's Puget Sound. In British Columbia's Clayoquot Sound, geoducks are just as abundant, living in tightly packed beds with four or five adult clams sharing a square foot of bottom sediment.

Geoducks are among the most valued seafood resources in the Northwest, with live specimens selling at retail prices of $10 to $20 a pound in the United States and considerably more overseas. For the past two decades they've been the focus of a carefully regulated, multimillion-dollar commercial fishery in both the United States and Canada.

For a much longer period, geoducks have been the recreational clam harvester's treasure as well as the seafood gourmet's delight. "I had been hearing about geoducks ever since first coming to Seattle," wrote Betty MacDonald in her 1945 best-seller *The Egg and I*. "People spoke of them with the mystic reverence usually associated with an eclipse of the sun or the aurora borealis."

Geoducks have established their worth in another way. As the "coal miner's canaries" of water quality, geoducks and other clams alert us to environmental threats from land-and water-based sources of pollution. Whenever a public beach is closed to clam digging, we should heed this early warning and take action to correct any problems from neighboring land or water uses—controlling erosion, curbing contamination from failing septic systems and other sources, and educating people to take more active roles in resource stewardship.

As a seasoned explorer of the West Coast's rocky, sandy, and muddy shores, I too have a "mystic reverence" for the geoduck clam. Whenever I visit the seacoast, I derive pleasure just from knowing that several feet beneath my waterproof boots lies an animal quite possibly 90 years my senior, silently finishing a supper of diatoms and algae inhaled through its meter-long neck.

In this, my fifth field guide for Sasquatch Books, I hope to provide a rare glimpse into the geoduck's strange and sedentary existence. Throughout, I've placed emphasis on feeding, breeding, and burrowing behaviors—those facets of a geoduck's life not easily observed in the field. Other sections of this guide are intended for use out-of-doors, to aid the reader in distinguishing this remarkable animal, King Clam, from the many smaller bivalves sharing its intertidal domain. For those with an epicurean interest in geoducks, I've included a section on preparing one's catch—the perfect end to a day on the soggy trail of the geoduck clam.

To create this guide, I've filter-fed on facts from authoritative works from other marine biologists, including Aven Mayer Anderson, Jr., Roland Anderson, Lynn Goodwin, Rick Harbo, and Eugene Kozloff. I am indebted to these scholars, as well as to my editor, Joan Gregory, for helping me to compile and shape the text.

I am also grateful for the book's sponsor, People for Puget Sound. This nonprofit organization has done much to protect the aquatic habitats and resources of Washington and British Columbia—ensuring that geoducks will continue to thrive in our seas. Partial profits from the sale of this book will help People for Puget Sound with its important mission.

Lastly, I wish to acknowledge my beloved companion, Mari F. Mullen, who gives me all my good ideas.

—David George Gordon

GEODUCK FAMILY TREE

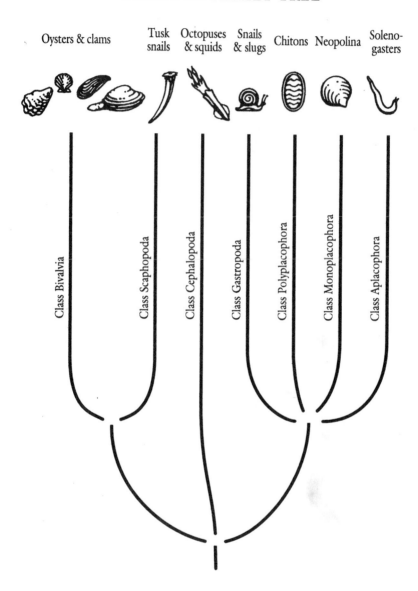

The Geoduck Family Tree

Well, he hasn't got a front and he hasn't got a back.
He doesn't know Donald, and he doesn't go "quack."

—Ron Konzak and Jerry Elfendahl,
"The Gooey Duck Song"

The geoduck (pronounced "gooey duck") is neither fish nor fowl. It is a mollusk, close relative of oysters, scallops, octopuses, squids, slugs, and snails. An estimated 100,000 species of mollusk currently inhabit our planet. Judging from the abundance of mollusk fossils in rocks from the Paleozoic era (620 million to 230 million years ago), this number represents a small fraction of the species that once filled the earth's ancient seas.

All mollusks, living and extinct, share some important characteristics. They are invertebrates (animals without backbones) with soft, unsegmented bodies. All mollusks pass through a stage in their early development characterized by the veliger larva, a minute planktonic form that is unique to members of this phylum. And all mollusks have the mechanisms, however reduced, for producing a hard outer shell made of calcium carbonate. In many molluscan species, this shell is quite elaborate, with distinctive spines, graceful whorls, and vivid colors. In others, the shell is vestigial or altogether absent, with only the shell-producing gland (called the mantle) to remind us that these nearly naked beings can claim membership in the mollusk clan.

The majority of living mollusks have been placed in two classes: *Bivalvia* (clams, mussels, oysters, and scallops) and *Gastropoda* (slugs and snails). Latin for "two-door," the term *bivalve* refers to the characteristic shell of these mollusks, which is divided into two sections (called valves), joined at one edge by a ligament hinge. Every bivalve wears one of these two-door coverings, for protection from predators and as a shield against the elements, both above and below the waterline.

With few exceptions, bivalves are sedentary animals. Employing glandular cement, sticky byssal threads, or a combination of the two holdfasts, these life-forms affix themselves to rocks, pilings, or other stationary objects. Other bivalves, including the geoduck, burrow into the substrate, and, unless they are dislodged by waves or currents, stay in one place for the length of their lives.

Wholly aquatic, bivalves have gills for breathing and tubelike siphons for sucking up food from the bottom or filtering food from the currents that wash over them. In marine habitats, both attached and burrowing bivalves may be exposed for brief periods at low tide. These dry-docked mollusks simply seal their valves to keep moisture in and wait to be inundated by the rising tide.

Around 31,000 species of bivalves fill niches in saltwater and freshwater bodies, as well as in estuaries and sloughs where the two waters meet. They are adapted to a wide range of environments—from cold mountain streams to tepid tropical reefs, polluted urban bays to pristine stretches of seacoast. In 1977, when marine scientists off the Galapagos Islands descended some 8,500 feet (2,600 m), they discovered an undersea oasis populated by two sizable but previously unknown bivalves— a mysterious 9½-inch (24 cm) white clam, *Calyptogena magnifica,* and a strange 7-inch-long (18 cm) mussel, *Bathymodiolus thermophilius*—both thriving on the sulfide-rich water flowing from thermal vents in the seafloor.

The largest bivalve is *Tridacna gigas,* the giant clam of the Indo-Pacific, which can weigh 650 pounds (295 kg) and grow to 5 feet (1.5 m) in length. This clam, whose valves have been used by island missionaries as baptismal fonts, filters plankton from the water column. At the same time, its bloodstream is fed glycerol and glucose—the high-energy products of photosynthesis—metered out by a crop of blue-green algae contained in pockets below the clam's skin.

Considerably smaller is the inch-long shipworm (*Teredo* or *Bankia* sp.), which bores holes into submerged, untreated wood. By slowly but steadily rotating its valves, the teredo carves a snug burrow for itself, all the while feeding on wood shavings produced in the process. During one exceptionally severe infestation that lasted from 1919 through 1920, teredos in San Francisco Bay gouged and gorged their way through about $21 million worth of wooden wharves, piers, and pilings. By riddling the wooden hulls of ships in the Spanish Armada, the ancestors of these industrious bivalves may have played a key role in Sir Francis Drake's 16th-century victory at sea.

Most bivalves, however, are neither monsters nor menaces. By conservative estimate, around 500 bivalve species now exist on the West Coast of North America; most of these are small "peace-loving" animals—shallow- and deepwater clams with valves no bigger than pistachio shells. There are also giants among the burrowers, the most massive being the geoduck (*Panopea abrupta*), the biggest burrowing clam in the world.

Geoducks have many smaller relatives scattered throughout the world: *Panopea aldrovandi* in the Mediterranean Sea and along the coast of Spain; *P. attenuata* from the coast of South Africa; *P. australis* and *P. zelandica* from Australia and New Zealand; *P. bitruncata* on the South Atlantic coast of North America; and *P. japonica* in Japan. Like the geoduck, these creatures are distinguished from other clams by their ponderous, elongate valves with irregular, concentric ribs, and by their large, double-barreled siphons, sheathed in a thin, leathery-looking outside layer of protein called the periostracum. However, they pale by comparison to *P. abrupta*—the real centerpiece of any clam-shell collector's display.

The Geoduck in Brief

KINGDOM: *Animalia*
PHYLUM: *Mollusca*
CLASS: *Bivalvia (Pelecypoda)*
ORDER: *Myoida*
SUPERFAMILY: *Hiatelloidea*
FAMILY: *Hiatellidae*
GENUS: *Panopea*
SPECIES: *abrupta* (formerly *generosa*)

SIZE
The largest burrowing clam in the world, attaining a shell length of at least 8.5 inches (21.6 cm) and a live weight (including the shell) of 7 pounds (3.2 kg). A few giants have been recorded at 14 and even 20 pounds (6.4 and 9 kg). In buried adults, the long contractile siphon may extend 39 inches (1 m) to reach the surface of the seabed.

RANGE
The West Coast of North America, from Alaska to Baja California.

HABITAT
Lower intertidal and subtidal zones of bays, sloughs, and estuaries, to depths of around 360 feet (110 m); most abundant between 30 feet and 60 feet (9.1 and 18.3 m) below the mean low tide mark; burrows in a variety of substrates, ranging from soft mud to pea gravel, mostly in stable mud or sand bottoms.

FOOD
Phytoplankton (single-celled marine algae), primarily diatoms and flagellate species.

EGGS
Minute (0.08 mm) ovals; up to 50 million from one female geoduck per year.

PREDATORS	Crabs, shrimp, sea stars, snails, fish, sea otters, and humans.
LIFE SPAN	Well over 100 years.

A Clam by Any Other Name

The word *geoduck* comes from the Nisqually tribe of Washington State, the original hunters of this clam and the earliest settlers of southern Puget Sound. They called their giant catch *gweduc*, a name that the first Europeans in the Northwest changed to gooeyduck or goeduck, the two alternate spellings most often used today. Over time, goeduck became geoduck—a linguistic switch that, in 1914, prompted the Federation of American Indians of the Northwest to adopt a resolution proclaiming "that the correct name of the large, edible clam... used for delicious food purposes and now miscalled 'geoduck' or 'goeduck' is 'gweduc,' meaning 'dig deep.' The word is from our native tongue and is not derived from the Chinook, Hudson's Bay Company English, or from the Greek or Italian."

This definitive statement from the Northwest tribes had no effect on changing the clam's name. Instead it motivated other Northwesterners to provide their own explanations for the geoduck's odd-sounding appellation. According to Carroll A. Gordon of Tacoma, Washington, the first white man to recognize the colossal clam was John F. Gowey, an avid duck hunter who would later become mayor of Olympia, Washington. On one occasion, Gowey returned from the field with a few large clams in his game bag. His detractors started calling these critters "Gowey's ducks." If one believes Gordon's story, the rest is history: the abundant supplies of Gowey's ducks are said to have influenced the selection of Olympia as Washington's state capital.

Settling on a mutually acceptable scientific name for the geoduck has been no piece of cake either, with a total of 14 different combinations of genus and species in use during this and the previous century. One outdated moniker, *Panopea generosa,* still appears in several popular guides to West Coast marine life. Outdated or not, it is considerably more appealing than *Panomya vaskuchevskensis,* a tongue twister of a name no longer in use. Another name, *Glycimeris generosa,* is translated literally as "sweet part of creation"—perhaps in reference to 19th-century naturalist Henry Hemphill's published claim: "the most delicious of any bivalve I have ever eaten, not excepting the oyster."

External Anatomy: Shell, Siphon, and Foot

Clams don't know what it's all about. They have no heads, so they do not bother with that sort of thing.

—Will Cuppy, *How to Attract the Wombat*

A geoduck's **shell** is rectangular, up to 9 or 10 inches (23 to 25 cm) long and 5 inches (13 cm) in height. Both **valves** are equally proportioned and sculpted with concentric but irregularly shaped growth lines. A small but prominent **ligament hinge** holds the two valves together. Whenever the geoduck contracts its large adductor muscles, drawing the two valves together in an attempt to close the shell, it places a strain on the elastic ligament hinge. When the muscles relax, presto: the springlike action of the ligament hinge serves to reopen the valves.

The valves' grayish white outside surfaces are covered by a thin, light-brown **periostracal covering.** This covering shields the shell's middle, or prismatic, layer of calcium carbonate crystals from scratches or abrasions—real drawbacks to a life spent in sand and gravel. The importance of such protection can be seen in the valves of older adult geoducks, where little of this periostracal covering remains.

The **periostracum** also keeps any carbon dioxide molecules in seawater from contacting the **prismatic layer** of the shell, a meeting that could cause this layer of shell to dissolve like an Alka Seltzer tablet in tap water. A third function of this periostracal skin has been suggested by marine invertebrate specialist D. Craig Edwards, who studied the carnivorous moon snail, *Polinices* sp., and its predation on the soft-shell clam, *Mya arenaria.* Edwards found that moon snails routinely focus their attacks on the thicker, periostracum-free areas of the shell valves—suggesting that something in the periostracal skin of the siphon may be repugnant to certain predators.

The constituents of the prismatic layer come from the geoduck's seawater bath, where there's no shortage of calcium carbonate or other mineral salts. In fact, seawater is supersaturated with these building materials. For this reason, the prismatic layer is always the most massive part of any marine bivalve's shell. In places, the geoduck's prismatic layer can be ½ inch (1.3 cm) thick.

Beneath the prismatic layer is the **inner nacre,** a thin veneer more widely known in other bivalve species as mother-of-pearl. It is from this layer that pearls are produced—a means of isolating and covering over any rough-edged and potentially abrasive particles that manage to insinuate themselves into the clam's

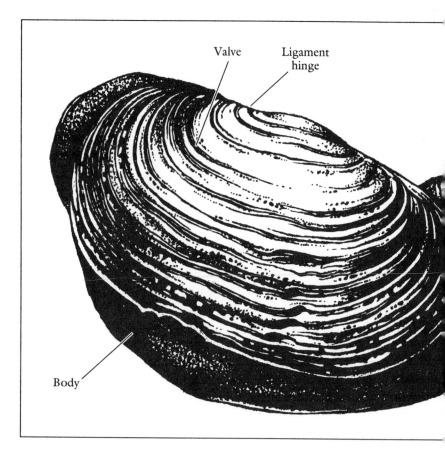

Valve   Ligament hinge

Body

soft insides. Nearly every bivalve, even the giant *Tridacna,* is capable of producing such natural gems. However, in the case of the geoduck and most other clam species, these concretions are chalky and lackluster—with more value as curiosities than as commodities. Goose bumps in geoduck shells (more politely described as **occlusions**) are actually pearls in the making, not fully separated from the shell's nacreous layer.

A geoduck's **siphon** is also known as its neck. This unusual appendage could more accurately be described as a tail, since it originates from the posterior end of the clam. Within this

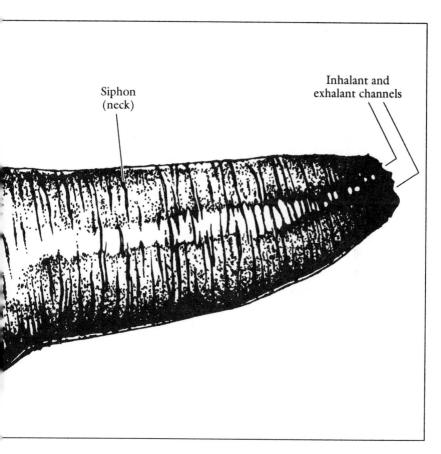

Siphon (neck)

Inhalant and exhalant channels

siphon are two long tubes—the geoduck's **inhalant** and **exhalant channels**. Both are enclosed in a sheath of muscle, which, in turn, is covered by a thin, coarse, wrinkly brown "skin"—made of a material that is similar to the shell's periostracal layer. This outer layer gives the geoduck's neck "l'aspect du penis d'un vieux cheval," to quote one 19th-century Frenchman, biologist F. Vles. To quote a more recent source, "It looks like something you *won't* see on TV."

An adult geoduck can extend its neck to a length of around 39 inches (1 m)—long enough for it to project 6 inches (15 cm) or more above the seafloor, enabling the deeply buried geoduck to respire and feed. The rounded tip of this long, phallic appendage is pierced by a pair of 1-inch (2.5 cm) holes—the openings to the two channels.

To escape predators, the geoduck can rapidly retract its neck, expelling a double-barreled blast of water through these innocuous-looking tubes. Once the geoduck senses that the coast is again clear, it sends the siphon back to the surface. This is accomplished by closing the holes in its siphon tip, then contracting the lateral muscles of the neck. As water pressure builds in the tubes, the siphon elongates until it attains its maximum length.

Body tissue accounts for most of the geoduck's heft. In fact, the fleshy **body** and fat, wrinkled neck are so large they cannot be fully withdrawn into the shell. The "open-door policy" of the portly geoduck is a sign that, at the sediment depth at which adult specimens live, few if any intruders must be shut out.

Far less conspicuous, particularly on adult geoducks, is the **foot**—an odd protuberance that, because of its shape, has given bivalves yet another classificatory title, the Pelecypoda or "hatchet-footed" animals. Young geoducks and many other kinds of clams use the foot to burrow into sand and sediments, alternately extending and contracting this muscular appendage to pull the rest of the animal downward. The valves clap shut after each extension of the foot, producing a jet of water that helps propel the clam. Sequential contractions of the foot muscles cause the geoduck's shell to rock back and forth, effectively plowing a path for the clam as it makes its way through the sediments.

Because the foot grows disproportionately with the rest of the clam, its value diminishes as a geoduck matures. The foot of an adult geoduck is roughly the size of an adult human's pinky finger. This degenerate digging device is so out of proportion that, if unearthed and placed on its side, the geoduck cannot right itself, let alone burrow into the substrate. Adult geoducks are homebodies, incapable, even if they want to, of moving out of the deep burrows in which they are permanently ensconced.

Internal Anatomy: Respiratory and Digestive Systems

Cut away a geoduck's shell and you won't see much—just the large, paired adductor and retractor muscles for closing the valves and operating the foot. Otherwise, this animal's insides seem to be little more than an amorphous pink glob. That's because nearly all of a clam's organs are hidden beneath its fleshy **mantle** and enveloped by a large, cream-colored glob of a **gonad.** As with all clams, male and female geoduck gonads are visually indistinguishable, requiring a microscope to tell the two sexes apart.

By snipping away the thick mantle tissue and probing within the gonadal mass, one can easily identify all of the geoduck's internal works: the heart in its pale pericardial cavity; the purple-hued gill filaments, draped over both sides of the visceral mass; and other vital organs like the stomach, liver, and intestine. Tucked away in a pocket, next to one of the intestine's many bends, is the brittle rod of digestive enzymes, called the **crystalline style.** As the style slowly dissolves, its enzymes flow into the geoduck's stomach, helping the clam break down its food.

Lining both inhalant and exhalant siphons are millions of specialized cells. Each of these cells is equipped with a lashlike filament called a **lateral cilium.** By waving these filaments in unison, the cells generate water currents, which flow down the inhalant siphon and bathe the clam's innards. Here a pair of gill sheets retrieve oxygen from the slow-moving water and transfer it to the bloodstream. The gills also release carbon dioxide and uric acid, cleansing the bloodstream of these metabolic by-products. Ciliary action inside the exhalant siphon carries these wastes out of the clam and into the great outdoors.

Geoduck **gills** also play a part in feeding. As water moves through the clam's guts, any phytoplankton (one-celled marine plants), zooplankton (minute marine animals), or other floating tidbits become trapped by the coating of mucus on each gill sheet. Both edible and inedible items are then passed by frontal cilia to the gills' outer edges, where they collect in special food grooves. Tiny fingerlike **labial palps**—literally translated as "lip appendages"—sort this stuff into different size categories. Unmanageably big or rough items accumulate at the edges of these palps. These discarded bits (called **pseudofeces**) and the strands of mucus that enshroud them are periodically coughed up, then chucked into the water column by way of the excurrent siphon, through violent spasms of the geoduck's muscular mantle. It's best not to be downcurrent of these!

More-digestible items are passed along to the geoduck's mouth and on to the esophagus and stomach, where they undergo further sorting. The choicest particles are broken down by digestive juices. Then the remaining waste products travel through the intestine to the anus and are passed to the outside world via the excurrent siphon.

Although detailed information about the geoduck's food intake is presently unavailable, there have been numerous studies of filter feeding in other, more easily cultured bivalves. In the 1930s, Dr. Paul Galtsoff of the U.S. Bureau of Fisheries (now the National Marine Fisheries Service) established that an Atlantic oyster strains water at a rate of about a gallon an hour, removing around 4 million planktonic organisms in the process. As these mollusks typically work an 18-hour shift, Galtsoff reasoned that a single oyster can strain as many as

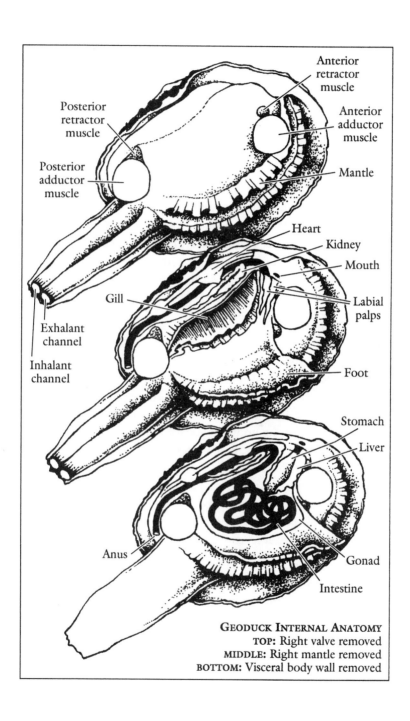

Posterior retractor muscle

Posterior adductor muscle

Anterior retractor muscle

Anterior adductor muscle

Mantle

Heart

Kidney

Mouth

Gill

Labial palps

Exhalant channel

Inhalant channel

Foot

Stomach

Liver

Anus

Gonad

Intestine

GEODUCK INTERNAL ANATOMY
TOP: Right valve removed
MIDDLE: Right mantle removed
BOTTOM: Visceral body wall removed

72 million planktonic organisms from the ocean each day. Along the Pacific Coast, where seasonal swarms of phytoplankton are exceptionally thick, it's a safe bet that in the same time period, at least this many organisms enter a geoduck's gut.

Geoduck Life Cycle

As so-called "broadcast spawners" (and blind ones at that), geoducks don't need to recognize members of the opposite sex. Like most marine mollusks, they simply release eggs and sperm into the water column, relying on waves and currents to bring the two genetic materials together. No parental involvement here: the fertilized eggs ride the same waves and currents, gradually developing, through successive larval stages, into little chips off the old block.

Geoducks release eggs and sperm several times in one spawning season—typically from late winter to early summer, with the greatest activity during May and June. Triggered by rising water temperatures and other cues from the environment, mature males release millions of free-swimming sperm. These sperm drift from the gonads and through the siphon's exhalant channel in smoky wisps, giving each protruding geoduck neck the look of a smoldering undersea volcano. The presence of sperm in the water stimulates mature female geoducks to start spawning, releasing as many as 5 million eggs at a time. These spherical white dots, each no bigger than a sand grain, drift out of the female through, you guessed it, the exhalant channel.

Females release as many as 10 batches of eggs each season, according to studies done at the Washington State Department of Fish and Wildlife's shellfish laboratory in the 1980s. Spawning of geoducks in the lab's tanks appeared to be cyclical, with the majority of females producing eggs every second or third week. This pencils out to around 50 million eggs per individual

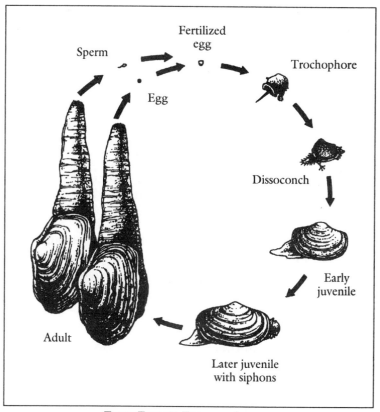

**FROM EGG TO ELDERLY ADULT:
140 YEARS IN THE MAKING**

per year. Now consider this: Egg production in female geoducks begins at age 4, and can continue to age 104. That adds up to around 5 billion eggs from one geoduck during its 100-year lifetime. It would take a million chickens more than 15 years to equal this output. Of course, the number of sperm released by male geoducks is easily several hundred times this amount. No wonder clam meat has an aphrodisiacal reputation!

Like all other mollusks, geoducks undergo a complex metamorphosis, dramatically taking new shapes several times in their first weeks of life. This remarkable transformation begins roughly 24 hours after geoduck eggs and sperm meet—a union that produces the **trochophore,** a ciliated larva barely visible to the naked eye. Its cilia act like tiny oars, propelling the top-shaped youngster through the plankton soup for the next two days.

Then the trochophore's body starts to change. It acquires an accessory organ—a ciliated, parachute-like **velum** for swimming—and a mantle, with which it begins to secrete a rudimentary shell. The tiny larva continues to grow, and its shell becomes more elaborate. Still less than 200 microns in diameter—half the size of a grain of salt—the larva is now called a **prodissoconch** or **veliger.**

Over a period of two to four weeks, the young geoduck is carried by waves and tidal currents in the upper water column, to new locales many miles from where it was born. Feeding on phytoplankton smaller than itself, it grows steadily. Many of its siblings will be gobbled up by copepods, larval fish, and other small planktonic animals. Along with a name change— from veliger to **dissoconch**—the geoduck larva loses its velum and swimming abilities, and sprouts a set of spines on the outer edges of its shell. It drops down from the upper water column and, settling on the seafloor, begins to act more like a grown-up clam.

Assisted by a newly formed foot, the dissoconch starts to crawl. Crawling is made easier by the dissoconch's **byssal threads**— adhesive guy lines secreted by a gland on the foot's outer surfaces that anchor the small clam to the sand grains around it. Releasing its hold on these grains, the dissoconch can "parachute" to new sites for settlement, pulled downcurrent by the drag created by the lines. At this stage in life, the foot does more than help the clam get around: its special ciliated cells also shovel food particles (primarily diatoms and bacteria) into the dissoconch's mouth.

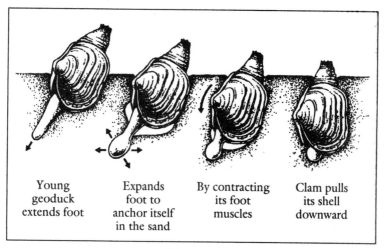

| Young geoduck extends foot | Expands foot to anchor itself in the sand | By contracting its foot muscles | Clam pulls its shell downward |

DIGGING

The next developmental stage begins when the dissoconch starts to dig with its foot. At first the clam—now the size of a grain of rice—cannot get very far down and may even return to the surface to parachute some more. But as the weeks pass, it slowly acquires the outward appearance and digging skills of a real clam. Now classified as a 1.5 mm to 7.5 mm **juvenile,** it plows deeper and deeper into the substrate, staying put with only its siphon tips exposed. Unlike its fleshy parents, this youngster can almost completely withdraw its body into its shell.

Juvenile geoducks continue to dig, reaching what biologists call a "refuge depth" of around 2 feet (61 cm)—beyond the reach of most clam predators—by the end of the second year. As they reach adult size and a maximum depth of 3 feet (91 cm), they become progressively more sedentary in nature. If unearthed, these stay-at-homes can no longer rebury themselves.

Mostly safe and secure in their burrows, adult geoducks devote their full energies to feeding, breathing, and breeding. All the while, the glands of the mantle continue to add fresh layers of shell. During the first 10 years of growth, these layers are added primarily to the outer edges of the shell. However, as the geoduck matures, new shell layers are added only to the shell's insides. Over subsequent decades, the material on the shell's outer edges is removed, slowly but steadily, by erosion. Thus elderly geoducks, like some people, gain weight and become shorter in their golden years.

Overall shell growth is fastest during spring and summer, when food is abundant and geoducks are most active. In winter months, shell-making slows. Food is scarce and geoducks throttle back on their life processes to conserve energy. There's good evidence that geoducks will actually retract their siphons and stop "breathing" during these months, relying on energy from anaerobic (oxygen-free) metabolism of glycogen stores.

Such seasonal fluctuations in shell growth reveal themselves as alternating bands in the shell walls. These light and dark bands can be read, like the rings of a tree, to determine a geoduck's age—proven in many instances to be well over 100 years. One specimen from Washington State was accurately assessed at 131 years of age, while another from the west coast of Vancouver Island was established at a mind-boggling 146 years. This places the geoduck in the company of such survivors as the tortoise or the sturgeon, whose life spans exceed 150 years. Alas, judging the ages of geoducks by their growth bands has a major drawback: before any counting can be done, the geoduck must surrender its shell, sacrificing its life in the name of science.

Who wouldn't like to learn the geoduck's secrets for long life? Such inside information is apparently shared by 50-year-old rock scallops (*Hinnites giganteus*) and 200-year-old *Tridacna* clams. Perhaps the key to longevity lies in the geoduck's stress-free existence, its ability to "keep clam" as the world turns. Or perhaps it's the simplicity of the geoduck's internal system, which, like a power lawn mower's single-cylinder engine, has few moving parts that can break or wear down. Whatever the cause, the result is exemplary: there may be geoducks alive today that were born when Abraham Lincoln was splitting rails.

Geoduck Predators

Of course, a geoduck's day-to-day existence isn't always a bed of roses, especially for juveniles, whose time on the seafloor is fraught with peril. The fragile shells of young geoducks are easily crushed by movements of the substrate, and burial by undersea mudslides and the natural settling of the sea bottom is always a threat. Small geoducks can also be smothered by layers of decaying algae and intertidal eelgrass. Should these clams come to the surface to breathe, they risk becoming easy targets for predatory sea life on the prowl.

Not yet fully buried, these young clams must elude an array of predators, including snails, sea stars, shrimp, and bottom-feeding fish. In laboratory tests, crabs have proven themselves to be particularly lethal: turned loose in two tanks containing 100 newly buried geoducks, three red rock crabs (*Cancer productus*) and three graceful crabs (*Cancer gracilis*) dug up and dispatched a third of their bivalve tankmates within 48 hours. Almost as well equipped for committing clamicide, giant moon snails (*Polinices lewisii*) use a rasping, tonguelike radula to drill holes in geoduck shells, through which they can suck out the meat.

Even fully buried adult geoducks are not entirely out of harm's way, as several marine animals, including the dogfish shark (*Squalus acanthias*) and Pacific staghorn sculpin (*Leptocottus armatus*) have learned to chow down on siphon tips. One cabezon fish (*Scorpaenichtys marmoratus*) was captured with

14 of these tasty bite-size morsels in its stomach. Whether the geoduck's siphon can regenerate a new tip has yet to be determined.

Deep-diving sea otters on the west coast of Canada's Vancouver Island and in the Aleutian Islands are known to dislodge and devour geoducks of all sizes. The fur coats of these mollusk-eating mammals come with convenient flaps of skin under each front leg for stashing clams and other small prey during a dive. This leaves the otter's paws free to hunt some more—a real plus for this voracious member of the weasel family, which, to stay warm in cold seas, must eat nearly a third of its weight in food each day.

A more passive approach is favored by the giant pink sea star (*Pisaster brevispinus*). This cold-blooded invertebrate prefers to position itself over a geoduck burrow and wait quietly for its meal to appear. When a clam extends its neck (as it inevitably must to procure oxygen and food and to excrete), *P. brevispinus* makes its move, seizing the tip with its sticky tube feet. By everting its stomach (a common feat among sea stars) and lowering its lining a foot or more into the geoduck's burrow, the patient predator can nibble on the hapless clam's neck. Shallowly buried geoducks are fair game for *P. brevispinus,* which, by extending its tube feet 2 feet (60 or so cm) down, can latch onto their shells and laboriously wrestle these geoducks from their limicolous lairs.

Like any other animals, geoducks are susceptible to disease. While studying the geoduck populations of Washington's Hood Canal in the late 1960s, Aven Mayer Anderson, Jr. found abnormal growths, perhaps attributable to fungal or protozoan infections, on the bodies of roughly 10 percent of his study specimens.

A final hazard is posed by pollution. As filter feeders, geoducks have the potential for accumulating pesticides, heavy metals, and other toxins suspended in their watery surroundings. While burrowing in bottom sediments, these clams can also come in contact with what are commonly called "hot spots"—localized buildups of pollutant-bearing particles beneath the sea—and succumb to the high contaminant levels.

A Few Geoduck Companions

Geoducks are solitary and sedentary by nature. However, they are guided by water currents to settle on suitable sediments near others of their kind. In some choice locales, there may be as many as 30 or 40 of these giant clams per square yard of seafloor. Here they share their submerged beds with other denizens of the deep.

One common geoduck neighbor is the tube-dwelling polychaete worm. These segmented worms dine on plankton, which they snag by a feeding apparatus that resembles an old-fashioned feather duster. The narrow, brown parchmentlike tubes of the polychaetes are preferred attachment areas for juvenile geoducks. Some researchers believe that chemicals from these tubes may trigger the metamorphosis of clam larvae, encouraging individual geoducks to stick around. How this benefits the worms has not been resolved.

Another geoduck neighbor, the sea pen (*Ptilosarcus gurneyi*), is also a plankton-eater, a Day-Glo orange relative of sea anemones and jellyfish that looks more like an ostrich plume than an invertebrate. A bulbous foot anchors this unusual animal in the mud and sand, while polyps on the sea pen's feathery upper body snare food from the water column. Polyps and other soft parts of the sea pen are brilliantly bioluminescent, giving off an eerie green light when shaken or stroked in the dark.

Two other invertebrates share an especially intimate relationship with the geoduck. These are two pea crabs of the genus

Pinnixa, which live their entire lives within the mantle cavities of both geoducks and horse clams. By living inside a clam, the crabs are guaranteed a cozy home plus ample nourishment from the "fallout"—the plankton and particles that geoduck siphons fail to suck up. When food is scarce, pea crabs will also snack on bits of body tissue abraded from their bivalve buddies.

The larger of the two pea crabs, *P. faba,* grows to an inch (2.5 cm) in diameter, while its relative, *P. littoralis,* seldom exceeds half an inch (1.3 cm). Females of both species are generally larger and less active than the males. Both sexes have poor eyesight, pigmentless bodies, and legs that are fairly useless for walking—just as you'd expect of a creature that prefers housekeeping inside a clam.

While several immature pea crabs may be found in one clam, only one adult male and one adult female take up permanent residence. Occasionally these freeloaders are expelled by the geoduck's spasmodic shudders. For some unknown reason, once outside the shell, these crabs are unable find their ways back home.

Clam Kin and Boring Relatives

Several different clam species inhabit the geoduck's muddy turf. Most easily confused with the geoduck are the **horse clams**—either *Tresus nuttallii,* also called the common gaper, or *T. capax,* a close relative from northern waters. Beach walkers may know these two bivalves as otter clams—a name that can be traced to the days when sea otter pelts were in high demand and fur hunters followed trails of *Tresus* shells to their clam-eating quarry. Both horse clam species coexist in Humboldt Bay, California, and in other locales along the coast.

More common intertidally in Oregon, Washington, and British
Columbia, *Tresus capax* specimens may reach 8 inches (20 cm)
in length and weigh as much as 4 pounds (1.8 kg). Their shells
are much more rounded than the geoduck's and can also be
distinguished by their noticeably more upswept posteriors.
Their leathery necks lack the geoduck's thick periostracum;
instead, they are covered
by coarse, wrinkled
skin. The tip
of *Tresus
nuttallii's*

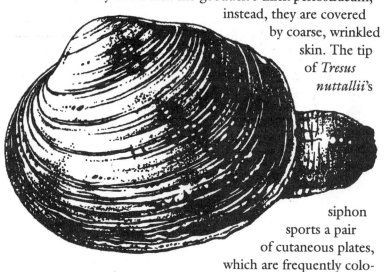

siphon
sports a pair
of cutaneous plates,
which are frequently colo-
nized by barnacles, seaweeds, and other forms of encrusting
life. The interior rim of the siphons of both species are ringed
by spiky tentacles, presumably to prevent large bits of debris
from being sucked into the clam's innards. When disturbed at
low tide, both horse clam species can spit jets of water 2 or 3
feet (up to 1 m) into the air.

Piddocks are world-champion borers that can excavate
and occupy holes in sandstone, concrete, and
even basalt rock. The 4-inch-long
(10 cm) Pilsbry or rough
piddock (*Zirfaea pilsbryi*)
is often mistaken for the
geoduck, whose siphons

are also similar in size. The color of the piddock's siphons (wine with white bumps) and their split tips are key characteristics for separating the borers from the burrowers. So is the piddock's fragile, multipart shell, the anterior of which sports a series of rough, rasping ridges.

Panomya chrysis is also called the **false geoduck**, because its choice of habitats and chunky 2¾-inch (7 cm) form so closely resemble those of the king of clams. But there are ways to tell the two bivalves apart. The valves of *P. chrysis* have a central concave section; the brownish orange siphon tubes are separated, not fused at the tip; and the opening to the inhalant tube is fringed with both inner and outer rows of tentacles. The opening to the exhalant tube contains an inner membrane— a device to concentrate and direct the outflowing current—that is lacking in the geoduck. Smaller than the geoduck, *P. chrysis* is also more plentiful in most subtidal areas.

Seldom mistaken for geoducks or, for that matter, each other are a handful of native clam species familiar to West Coast diggers and diners. These are the bent-nosed clams (*Macoma nasuta*), butter clams (*Saxidomus giganteus*), Pismo clams (*Tivela stultorum*), and razor clams (*Siliqua patula*).

The smallest of the four, the **bent-nosed clam** has a flattened shape. The posterior ends of its 2-inch-long (5 cm) valves are distinctively flexed, giving the clam its bent-nosed appearance. A pair of separated orange siphons protrude through this bend. Bent-nosed clams can tolerate a wide range of conditions, enabling them to settle in sandy bays, on mudflats, and even between cobbled stones on rocky coasts.

The **butter clam's** range extends from Alaska to Humboldt Bay, California, where, along some coasts, the 4-inch-long (10 cm) bleached white valves frequently litter the beaches. Live specimens bury themselves deep—nearly a foot (30 cm) into the mud and sand. A key ingredient of chowders and seafood stews, these clams have been harvested commercially throughout their range for many decades.

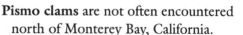

Pismo clams are not often encountered north of Monterey Bay, California. Their heavy, 6-inch-long (15 cm) shells are unusually glossy, as if a good coat of varnish had been applied to both valves. The short siphons of these clams are obvious clues that Pismos make their homes in the first few inches of beach sand, where they are easily retrieved by clam diggers.

By necessity, 6-inch-long (15 cm) **razor clams** are perhaps the fastest burrowing bivalves. Narrow, streamlined valves and a remarkably muscular foot are put to good use on exposed ocean beaches, where this surf dweller must frequently rebury itself after each incoming wave. This bivalve's ability to burrow makes razor clamming a high-energy sport. "If the clam is missed on the first effort, it is well to try for another one," suggests Canadian D. B. Quayle in

The Intertidal Bivalves of British Columbia, "for the one missed will have dug itself so deep that it may be obtained only by a considerable excavation."

Several species of clam have been accidentally and intentionally introduced into the geoduck's range. Some of these non-natives were brought here in shipments of oyster "seed," purchased from aquaculturists in Japan and the Far East. Today, stowaways like *Venerupis phillippinerum*, the **Japanese littleneck** (or Manila) **clam,** have fully acclimated to West Coast life.

A handful of non-native clams may have been intentional transplants, perhaps introduced by amateur and professional shellfish harvesters in fairly recent times. These include the **eastern soft-shell clam** (*Mya arenaria*), common in the northeastern United States but entirely absent from old shell middens of Northwest Coast tribes, and the **quahog** (*Mercenaria mercenaria*), the geoduck's Atlantic coast counterpart whose purple-and-white shell was made into wampum—the common currency of New England tribes. While eastern soft-shell clams have adapted to their new environs, quahogs have never really taken hold. According to Eugene N. Kozloff, author of *Seashore Life of the Northern Pacific Coast,* most live quahogs in San Francisco Bay are actually recently imported specimens from the East Coast that have been discarded or have fallen out of holding pens. Breeding populations of quahogs still exist in Humboldt Bay and also in Colorado Lagoon, near Long Beach, California, several decades after their introduction to these locales.

The Subsistence Fishery

In her 1940 monograph, Columbia University anthropologist Marian W. Smith described the shellfish that were harvested seasonally by the Nisqually tribe. These included the geoduck and four other clams: the horse clam, butter clam, rock clam (*Protothaca staminea,* also called the native littleneck), and another species, described as an intermediate between the horse clam and the geoduck, for which no English name was known. This nameless bivalve, according to Smith, "had a neck not quite so long as the gwiduck [*sic*] and a shell more oval than that of the horse clam, into which its entire body fit." This description fits the eastern soft-shell clam (which probably was well-established by the time of Smith's study) to a T.

The Nisqually and other Northwest coastal tribes gathered geoducks with a 4-foot-long digging stick fashioned of maple or cherry wood. Both ends of this stick were sharpened and fire-hardened, and one end was often carved to give it a slight scoop. The effectiveness of such a simple implement can be verified by the mountains of discarded clam shells comprising kitchen middens at abandoned Northwest coast villages.

During spring and summer months, native American women devoted much of their time to digging and processing shellfish. To lighten their workloads, they developed an ingenious method for cleaning their catch. Clams were put in open, birdcage-weave baskets made from the roots and bark of cedar and spruce trees. The baskets were then suspended in seawater, so the clams would be purged of sand and mud by incoming and outgoing tides.

While some clams were eaten fresh, most geoduck necks were smoked and stored for future consumption. "As a rule these clams kept as well as smoked salmon and, in the same way, were regarded as economic items to be accumulated and traded," wrote Smith. The Nisqually and other coast-dwelling tribes prepared clam chowders in winter months, using dried, powdered clams for a base. In one traditional recipe, clams were pulverized, then simmered in bentwood boxes or baskets filled with hot water. Wild onions and dried seaweed helped season the chowder; only with the arrival of European settlers and their crops did native Americans add potatoes, celery, carrots, salt, pepper, and a particular favorite—bacon fat— to their geoduck chowders and stews.

Recreational and Commercial Harvests

Thousands Out for Elusive Geoducks on Nearby Beaches; Day Island Residents Report Private Property Overrun by Clam Diggers; Owners Protest; Big Demand for Boats as Hunters With Shovels and Buckets Take Advantage of Extreme Low Tides

—headline, the *Tacoma Ledger,* May 22, 1932

European settlers of the Pacific Northwest were aware of the geoduck's nutritive and economic importance. They sold their catches, along with other clams, in the markets of Olympia, Washington, and Portland, Oregon. In the 1880s, the U.S. Fisheries Commission tried to transplant geoducks on the Atlantic shore, shipping seed stocks by steamboat. Later, plans were made to transport live geoducks by the recently completed Transcontinental Railroad. Neither attempt proved feasible, and geoducks were never successfully introduced outside their natural range.

For nearly 100 years, a small but enthusiastic recreational shellfish fishery flourished on the West Coast. But by the mid-1920s, geoduck stocks in many shoreline locales had noticeably declined. Fearing that the fishery might make the geoduck extinct, the Washington State legislature made it illegal to take or even possess these clams. This prohibition remained in effect until 1931, when new regulations were enacted, permitting geoducks to be taken for personal use, but preventing anyone from canning or selling them. The new regulations also provided that "no one person shall at any time maim or injure the geoduck or thrust any stick or other instrument through the neck or body of such geoduck before digging."

Unfortunately, the legislature's attempts to rebuild the dwindling recreational geoduck fishery were in vain. By the late 1940s once-profuse stocks of geoduck in Washington's intertidal zones had been depleted. On one Northwest beach after the next, local diggers began turning their attentions to less enticing but more predictably obtained horse clams and butter clams.

Then, in the 1960s, new information gave the torpid geoduck fishery a jolt. While retrieving dummy practice torpedoes from submarines in Hood Canal, U.S. Navy divers chanced upon a submerged field of double-barreled siphons, thus gaining the first good glimpse of subtidal geoduck reserves. With a grant from the U.S. Bureau of Fisheries, workers with Washington State Department of Fisheries (now Washington State Department of Fish and Wildlife) began to systematically survey and characterize this new resource in Washington's Puget Sound.

Encouraged by data from these surveys, the state of Washington initiated a commercial geoduck harvest program in 1970—

the first such operation in the world. In the fishery's first year, more than 40 tons (37 metric tons) of geoducks were harvested from subtidal beds throughout Puget Sound. Seven years later, an all-time record catch of 4,323.3 tons (3,922 metric tons) was landed. Leases to geoduck tracts are now sold at auction, and the money—around $20 million per year —is reinvested in aquatic lands enhancement and geoduck research projects. Ongoing surveys of geoduck abundance and conservative catch quotas (no more than 2 percent of the state's legally fishable geoducks can be taken each year) ensure that this valuable resource will sustain itself in perpetuity.

Born in 1976 on the east coast of Vancouver Island, the British Columbia geoduck fishery is now the province's most lucrative invertebrate harvest operation, valued at around $23 million in 1993 and $34 million in 1994. With the fairly recent demand for live geoducks by Asian seafood connoisseurs, the wholesale price per pound has skyrocketed from 30 cents in 1987 to nearly $8 in 1994.

Commercial geoduck harvesters wear insulated dive suits to shield them from the cold. They carry super-size waterpicks (called "stingers"), attached to hoses that can deliver 100 pounds (45.4 kg) of water pressure—ample force to loosen even the most deeply entrenched clams. The divers usually breathe through long, flexible tubes, supplied with air from shipboard compressors.

Thus outfitted, commercial harvesters can remain on the bottom for many hours at a time, scanning the seafloor for "shows"—the tell-tale dimples made by the geoducks' retracting siphons—or flushing bivalves from their burrows. Working at top speed, an experienced "duck diver" can usually harvest two large clams per minute, or as many as five in exceptionally dense beds. Hoisted to the surface in cargo nets, the geoducks are gently packed in plastic milk crates, stacked several deep on the harvest boat's deck. Unloaded at a shellfish plant, the live geoducks are cushioned in bubble wrap or other protective packing materials, then trucked to domestic markets or flown to outlets in Taiwan, Hong Kong, or Japan.

Finding Geoducks in the Wild

The most robust geoducks are usually found in sandy, muddy, or mixed substrates, where water currents are swift, and at depths of 30 to 60 feet (9 to 18 m), where the clams' favorite food, phytoplankton, is abundant. Adults and juveniles also settle in pea gravel and among piles of cobbled rock. Small adults with stunted siphons are probably ones that have encountered barriers to their burrowing and, as a result, have been forced to live in the first 1 or 2 feet (less than 1 m) of sea sediments. Areas of exceptional abundance include Washington's Puget Sound, inhabited by an estimated 130 million geoducks (the largest mass of any marine animal in this region) and British Columbia's Clayoquot Sound, populated in places by as many as 40 geoducks per square yard— a veritable geoduck convention, if you will.

Populations in California, Oregon, and Alaska are considerably smaller, limited to a few sloughs and embayments with favorable conditions. In California the most accessible of these is Elkhorn Slough National Estuarine Research Reserve, a federally protected oasis for intertidal life, near the coastal town of Moss Landing. In Oregon, geoducks are most predictably obtained on the beaches of Netarts Bay.

Several areas with high geoduck abundance have been closed to commercial and recreational shellfish harvesting because of pollution. Most of these areas are near the outfalls of urban sewer systems, which have historically discharged wastewater without treatment. While potentially harmful to any humans who eat the tainted clam meat, such pollution does not appear to be harming the geoducks: beds containing millions of geoducks are located north and south of Seattle's wastewater treatment facility at West Point.

Since 1991 thousands of captively reared juvenile geoducks have been transplanted by Washington State Department of Fish and Wildlife volunteers on the beaches of Kopachuck, Fay Bainbridge, Kitsap Memorial, and Hope Island State Parks. Clam diggers have been asked to treat these new "geoduck gardens" with care and to let the new transplants grow to maturity. If all goes as planned, these once overharvested beaches could become the best sites for close encounters with the Brobdingnagian bivalves.

'Duck Digging How-Tos

"One of the best things about clam digging is that captured mollusks don't look at you with reproachful eyes," wrote Dolly Connelly of Port Townsend, Washington, in a 1975 issue of *Pacific Search* magazine. "They don't whimper and they can't be petted. Besides, they fight back, squirting cold water up your pant leg and clinging pugnaciously to their cold, wet burrows."

Geoducks can be observed in winter on many Pacific beaches, when ocean storms wash away beach sands, bringing these buried treasures a bit closer to the surface. Because the lowest winter tides occur at night, flashlights or lanterns are essential. So are foul-weather gear or other kinds of warm, waterproof apparel. Hip waders or knee-high rubber boots, preferably with good traction for rock hopping, are also advisable.

In his comprehensive beachcomber's guide, *Stalking the Blue-Eyed Scallop*, Euell Gibbons suggests scheduling a geoduck field trip for late October or early November, approximately two days after the full of what Northwest Coast Indians call the

GEODUCK HARVESTING TOOLS

"Mad Moon." On these evenings, the outgoing tides reach their lowest ebb, revealing shoreline stretches that at most other times of the year are inundated by several feet of seawater. "I know it sounds like a psychotic sorcerer's formula to say the Geoduck must be sought at midnight, just two days after the full of the Mad Moon, but it happens to be a sober fact," the world-famous forager notes.

The extremely low midday tides of early summer also offer opportunities for geoduck watchers. However, these tides tend to lure more people to public beaches, many of whom are intent on capturing the very creature you seek. For this reason, it may be wise to limit your shellfish surveys to the more remote stretches of seashore. Intensively harvested in past decades, geoducks are seldom numerous on any West Coast beach. Direct your attention to the exposed areas that are farthest from shore, and watch for the three S's—squirts, siphons, and shows.

Of course, even after you've located a geoduck, you're likely to get just a fleeting glimpse. A swiftly withdrawn siphon and the shower of water such an action will produce often give the impression that the geoduck is racing down through the substrate to elude capture. Beach walkers must remind themselves that adult geoducks are actually homebodies, more or less permanently fixed in their deep burrows. They must also resist the temptation to grasp this fleeing tube of flesh or to wrestle the geoduck out of the sand by its siphon. Such maneuvers usually cause the siphon to snap in two— a lose-lose situation for you and the clam.

Should you care to collect a geoduck for observation or gustation, bring a shovel and a tubular metal "geoduck gun," 4 feet (1.2 m) long and 16 or more inches (40.6+ cm) in diameter. Some clam diggers claim success with a metal trash can from which the bottom has been removed. Both tube and trash can will serve the same purpose—to keep beach sand and mud from refilling the hole you must dig.

Having located a siphon or show, jam the end of the tube into the sand around it. By twisting and rocking the tube, you should be able to work it into the sediment. The deeper the better: remember, there's a clam way down there! Now use the shovel to gently excavate the sand, taking care to avoid damaging the geoduck's shell. As you near the 3-foot (1 m) depth, reach into the tube and feel around for the shell. Once you locate this prize, rock the geoduck back and forth, releasing its hold on the muddy warren. You can now remove the tube and claim your clam. If the sole objective of one's trip to the beach is to study the biggest burrowing bivalve at close range, then any captured specimens should be returned to the sediments, their necks pointing upward, buried at the appropriate depth.

For the sake of the many other intertidal creatures (including juvenile geoducks) that have been disturbed in the digging, be sure to refill the hole you've just made. On every beach outing, bring a bag to pick up any paper, glass, metal, or plastic trash that you find. And always observe state or provincial bag limits. Far from capricious quotas, these limits have been thoughtfully determined to ensure the long-term survival of certain shellfish species. Shellfish harvest restrictions for Alaska, British Columbia, Washington, Oregon, and California are presented on page 46 of this book.

Preparing Your Catch

Before collecting any geoducks for personal consumption, clam diggers should consult their state or provincial fish and wildlife department or health department for up-to-date infor mation about so-called red tides—seasonal blooms of the toxin-producing phytoplankton species *Gonyaulax catenella*. While filter feeding in waters with these blooms, clams and other bivalves can accumulate the toxin. Eating clams with high levels of this toxin can cause diners to succumb to a condition commonly known as paralytic shellfish poisoning (PSP). Early physical symptoms of PSP include tingling and numbness of the lips and tongue. Depending on the quantity of toxin consumed, these early warning signs may progress to tingling of the fingers and toes, difficulty breathing, and loss of control in the arms and legs. In extreme cases, death can occur when the respiratory system becomes paralyzed. The effects of PSP are worst when clams are eaten on an empty stomach. Several

West Coast states operate toll-free PSP hotlines to inform shellfish harvesters of recent shellfishing closures due to local *Gonyaulax catenella* blooms (see the list on page 48).

Geoducks taken for food should be cleaned and eviscerated within a few days of their capture. To prepare a geoduck for eating, use a sharp knife to sever the abductor muscles and remove the shell. Make a cut around the intestines and gonads, trimming off visceral membranes. Wash the body under running water—the best way to remove any grit or sand.

Next, scald the siphon in boiling water. When it has cooled, peel away the periostracum. Vigorously scrub the siphon with a vegetable brush to remove any dark coloration. The substrate in which a geoduck settles will affect the color of its meat; individuals from mud bottoms are darker and less visually appealing than ones from pea gravel or cobbled rock habitats, particularly to Asian customers, who traditionally shop for seafood with their eyes.

Now separate the siphon from the body meat, severing it at the base. The geoduck is now ready for use in your favorite recipe —baked in layers with steamed spinach and grated cheese; cut into strips, dipped in beaten egg and cracker crumbs, and sautéd lightly in butter; stewed in tomato sauce, along with vegetables and bits of andouille sausage; or served raw atop seasoned rice ovals, touched lightly with wasabi. The delicate flavor of this versatile clam adapts well to most crabmeat or oyster recipes and makes an excellent chowder.

Savor every bit of your meal: it probably took the geoduck a dozen years (or more like several dozen) to produce the main ingredient—its tasty flesh.

To Learn More About Geoducks

BOOKS AND REPORTS

Goodwin, Lynn, and Pease, Bruce. *Pacific Geoduck Clam.* (U.S. Fish and Wildlife Service Biological Report 82 (11.120), TR EL-82-4, December 1989.)

Kozloff, Eugene. *Seashore Life of the Northern Pacific Coast.* (Seattle: University of Washington Press, 1983.)

Quayle, D.B. *The Intertidal Bivalves of British Columbia.* (Victoria: British Columbia Provincial Museum, 1970.)

Russell-Hunter, W. D. *A Life of Invertebrates.* (New York: MacMillan Publishing Co., Inc., 1979.)

ARTICLES

Carmichael, Suzanne. "Around Seattle, an Oversize Clam Shines in Sushi," *The New York Times,* November 22, 1992.

Connelly, Dolly. "By Any Name, Gweducs are Real," *Pacific Search,* March 1975.

Milne, Lorus J. and Margery J. "We Go Gooeyducking," *Natural History,* April 1948.

Stuller, Jay. "King of the Clams," *Wildlife Conservation,* June 1995.

Geoduck Harvest Regulations
(as of December 1995)[1]

ALASKA

Alaska Department of Fish and Game
Division of Sport Fish
P.O. Box 95526
Juneau, AK 99802-5526
(907) 465-4180

Recreational geoduck harvesters in all areas of Alaska are required to obtain a sportfishing license. Individuals 60 years or more in age or less than 16 years of age are exempt from these license requirements. State residents may harvest six geoducks per trip; nonresidents are prohibited from participating in this harvest. The season is open throughout the entire year. Approved gear for collecting geoducks includes shovels and manually operated clam guns. It is unlawful to buy, sell, trade, or barter geoducks or their parts collected for personal use.

BRITISH COLUMBIA

British Columbia Department of Fisheries and Oceans
Nanaimo Area Office
60 Front Street
Nanaimo, BC V9R 5H7
(604) 754-0230

Prior to 1995, recreational geoduck diggers in British Columbia were restricted to an "aggregate bag limit" of 75 clams per person per day. New regulations for the recreational geoduck fishery were being drafted as this book went to press. Resource managers anticipate that these regulations will be approved in late 1996. Until then, British Columbia's recreational geoduck fishery is closed.

[1]Please consult the appropriate regulatory entity for updates.

WASHINGTON

Washington Department of Fish and Wildlife
600 Capitol Way N
Olympia, WA 98501-1091
(360) 902-2200

A Personal Use Shellfish License is required for all recreational geoduck harvesting. The fishery is open year-round, and there is no limit on size. A daily bag limit of three geoducks per person has been established. Clams can be dug by hand or by hand-operated fork, pick, or shovel. Each digger must use a separate container; however, digging equipment may be shared. It is unlawful to possess only the neck of a geoduck.

OREGON

Oregon Department of Fish and Wildlife
Marine Region
2040 Marine Science Drive
Newport, OR 97365
(503) 867-4741

There is presently no significant recreational geoduck fishery on the Oregon coast, nor are there license requirements for recreational shellfish harvesting within the state. Geoducks are regulated as "miscellaneous clams," with a per-person limit of the first 36 geoducks taken—a nearly impossible feat during a single low-tide occurrence.

CALIFORNIA

California Department of Fish and Game
P.O. Box 944209
Sacramento, CA 94244-2090
(916) 653-7664

A Nonresident Sport Fishing License, Resident Sport Fishing License (Ocean Only), or One-Day Sport Fishing License are required of any recreational geoduck harvester 16 years or older. The daily bag limit of three geoducks per person must be observed, with the first three geoduck clams retained, regardless of size or broken condition. Geoducks and other clams may be dug from one half-hour before sunrise to one half-hour after sunset. Spades, shovels, hoes, rakes, or other hand-operated tools are allowed.

PSP (Red Tide) Hotlines

Contact the following organizations for up-to-date information about PSP (paralytic shellfish poisoning) and shellfish-harvesting closures.

ALASKA: Check with the local Department of Environmental Conservation office.

BRITISH COLUMBIA: Fisheries and Oceans' Shellfish and Red Tide Update, (604) 666-3169.

WASHINGTON: Washington State Department of Health PSP Hotline, (800) 562-5632.

OREGON: Oregon Department of Agriculture's Shellfish Information Line, (503) 986-4728.

CALIFORNIA: California Department of Health Services' Shellfish Information Line, (510) 540-2605.